Book 2 - Piano/Guitar Accompaniment

STANDARD OF EXCELLENCE

COMPREHENSIVE BAND METHOD

By Bruce Pearson

ABOUT THE ACCOMPANIMENTS

This book includes piano accompaniments and chord symbols for all full band exercises in STANDARD OF EXCELLENCE, Book 2. Use these accompaniments to enhance practice sessions, or as an accompaniment when performing as a soloist or with other band members.

These accompaniments are also available fully orchestrated on both compact disc and cassette tape:

▶ Book 2 Accompaniment CDs — 2 CD set including all accompaniments (W22CD).

▶ Book 2 ENHANCER KIT — 2 CD set including all accompaniments, plus iPAS™ practice and assessment software (PW22EK).

▶ Book 2 Accompaniment CD — Part 1 only (W22CD1).
▶ Book 2 Accompaniment CD — Part 2 only (W22CD2).

▶ Book 2 Accompaniment Cassette — Part 1 only (W22CT1).
▶ Book 2 Accompaniment Cassette — Part 2 only (W22CT2).

ISBN 0-8497-5972-2

© 1994, 2005 Neil A. Kjos Music Company, 4382 Jutland Drive, San Diego, California.
International copyright secured. All rights reserved. Printed in U.S.A.
WARNING! Governments around the world provide copyright laws to encourage composition and publication of new music.
Anyone copying this music without permission is breaking the copyright law and is subject to penalties.
Please do not violate copyright laws. Do not copy or reproduce the contents of this book in any way. **Thank you!**

kjos NEIL A. KJOS MUSIC COMPANY, PUBLISHER

W22PG

2

2 **CONCERT B♭ MAJOR SCALE SKILL**

3 **BOTANY BAY**

Australian Folk Song

4. DRIVE TIME

Andante

5. SHEPHERD'S HEY

English Folk Song

Moderato

6. CONCERT E♭ MAJOR SCALE SKILL

7. MOLLY MALONE

Irish Folk Song

8 NO LOOKING BACK

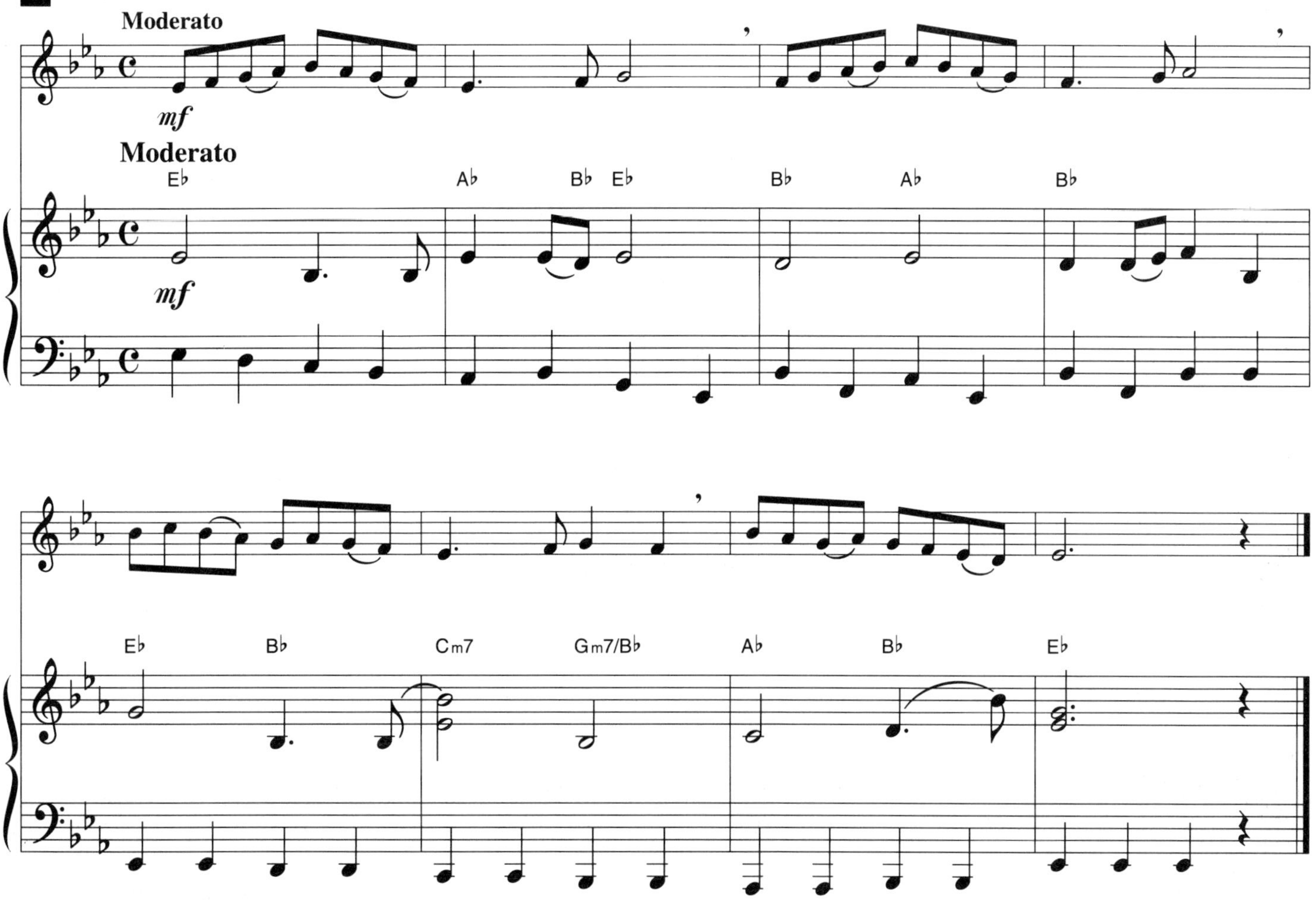

9 TURKISH MARCH

Wolfgang Amadeus Mozart (1756 - 1791)

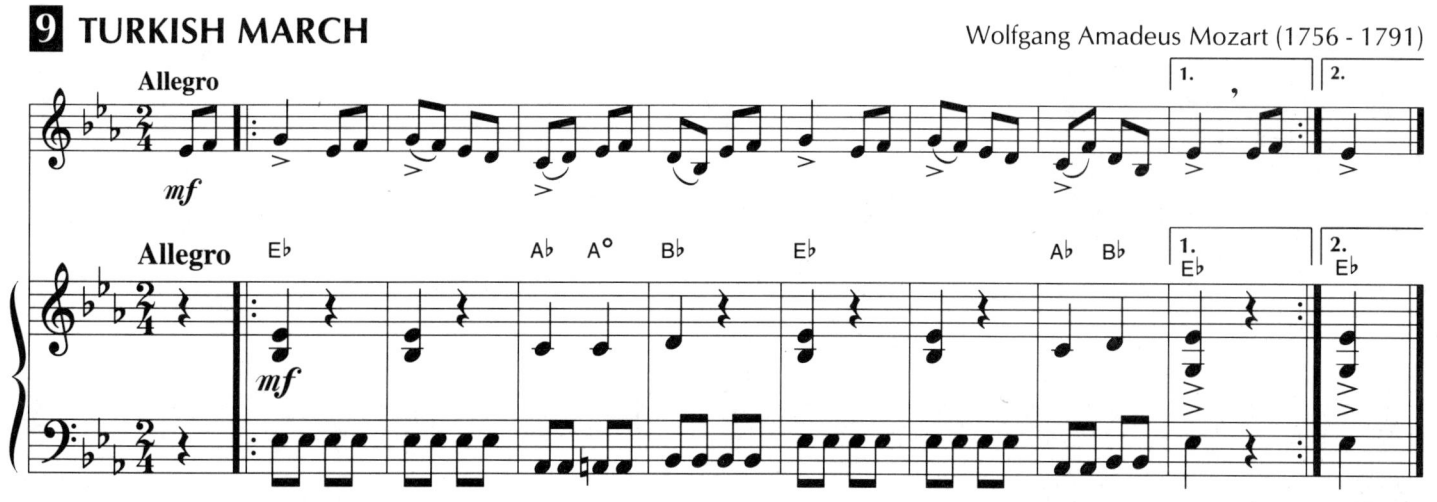

14 GIVE ME THAT OLD TIME RELIGION

American Spiritual

17 SYNCOPATION SENSATION

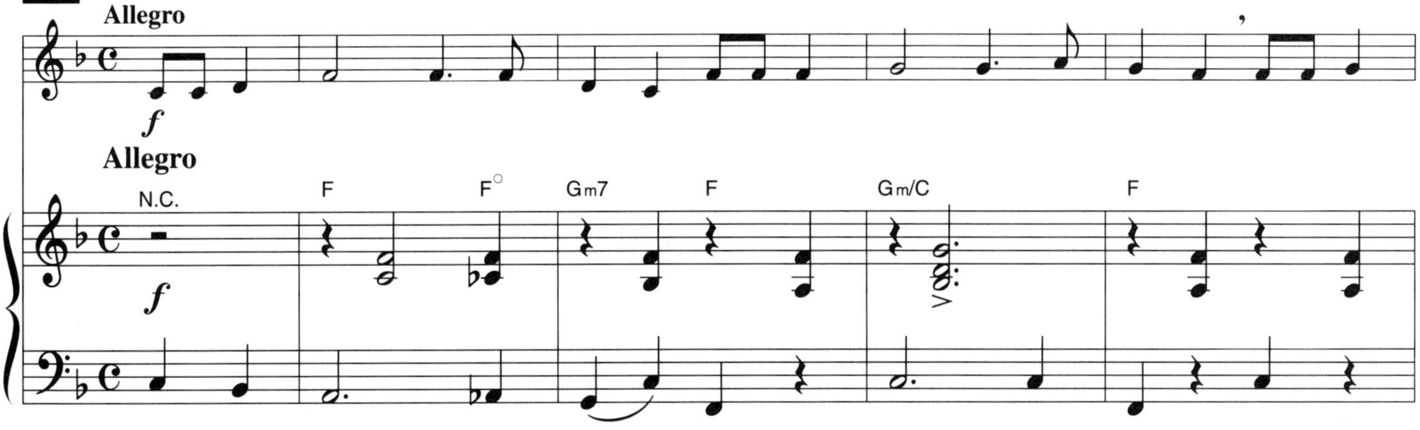

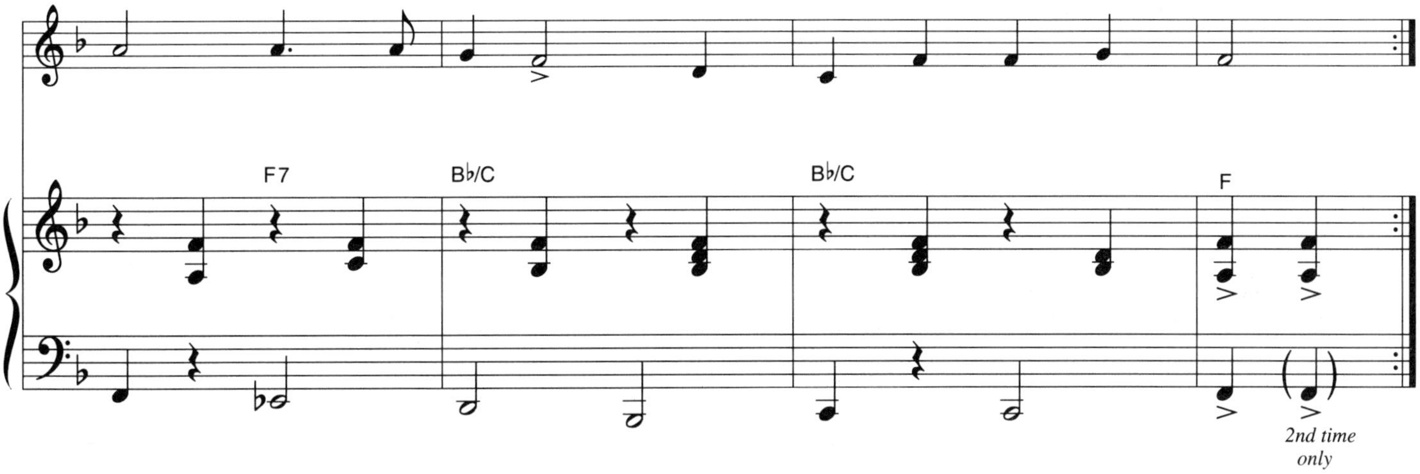

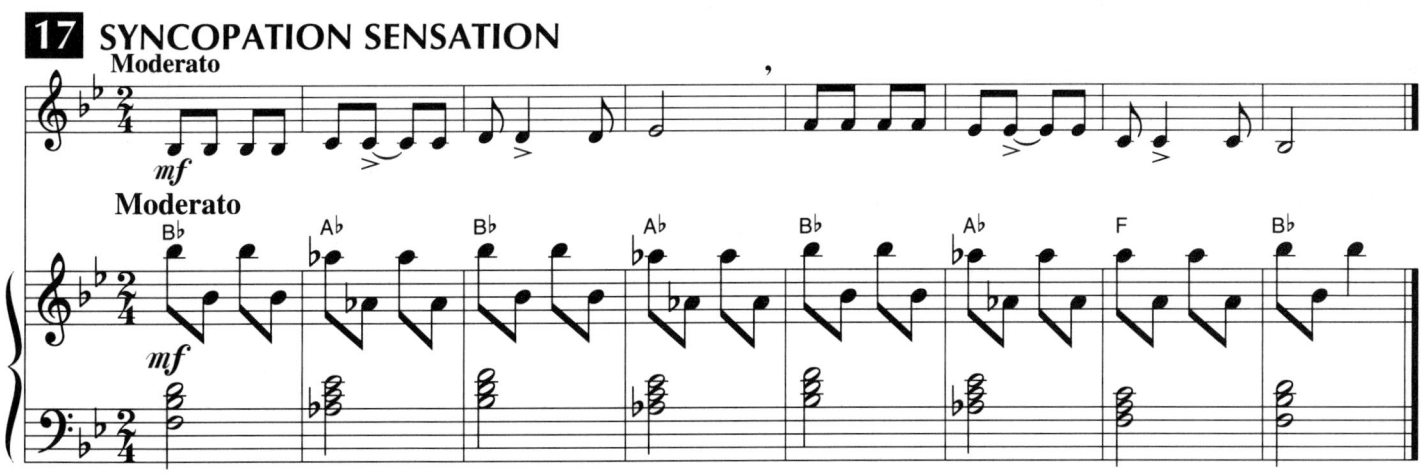

18. THE RIDDLE SONG

American Folk Song

19. NOBODY KNOWS THE TROUBLE I'VE SEEN

American Spiritual

29. GO FOR EXCELLENCE!

30. EIGHTH REST ON THE BEAT

31. EIGHTH REST OFF THE BEAT

34 YANKEE DOODLE - Duet

American Folk Song

36 CONCERT A♭ MAJOR SCALE SKILL

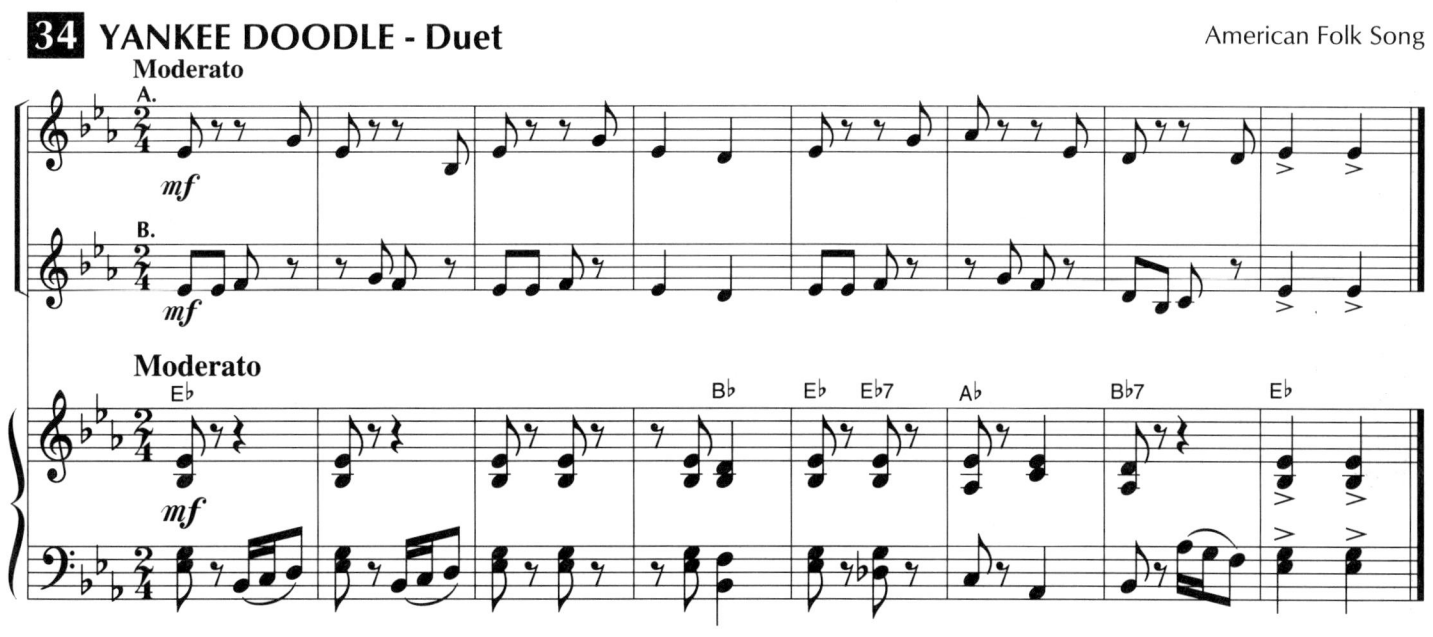

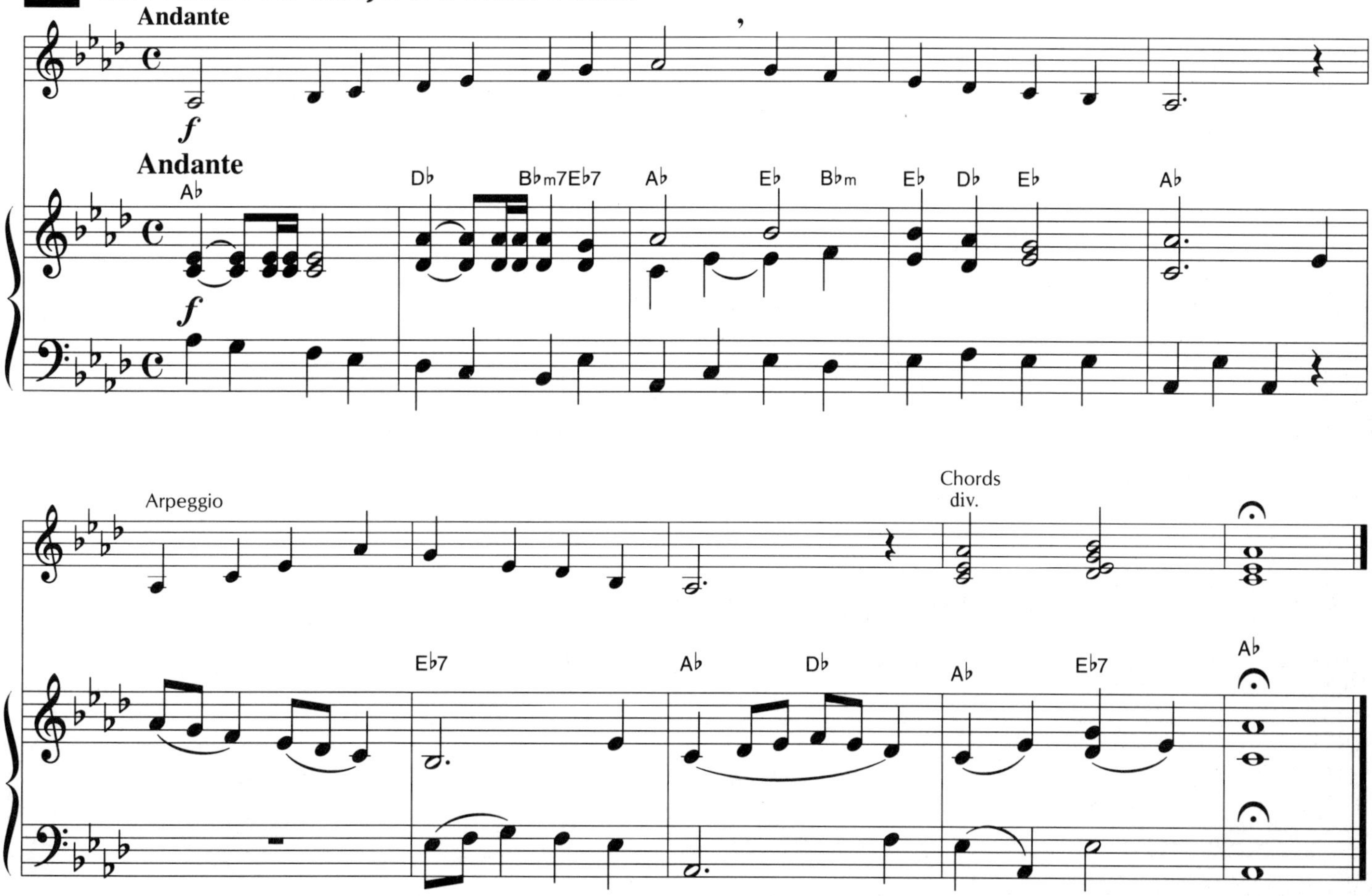

37 GREASED LIGHTNING

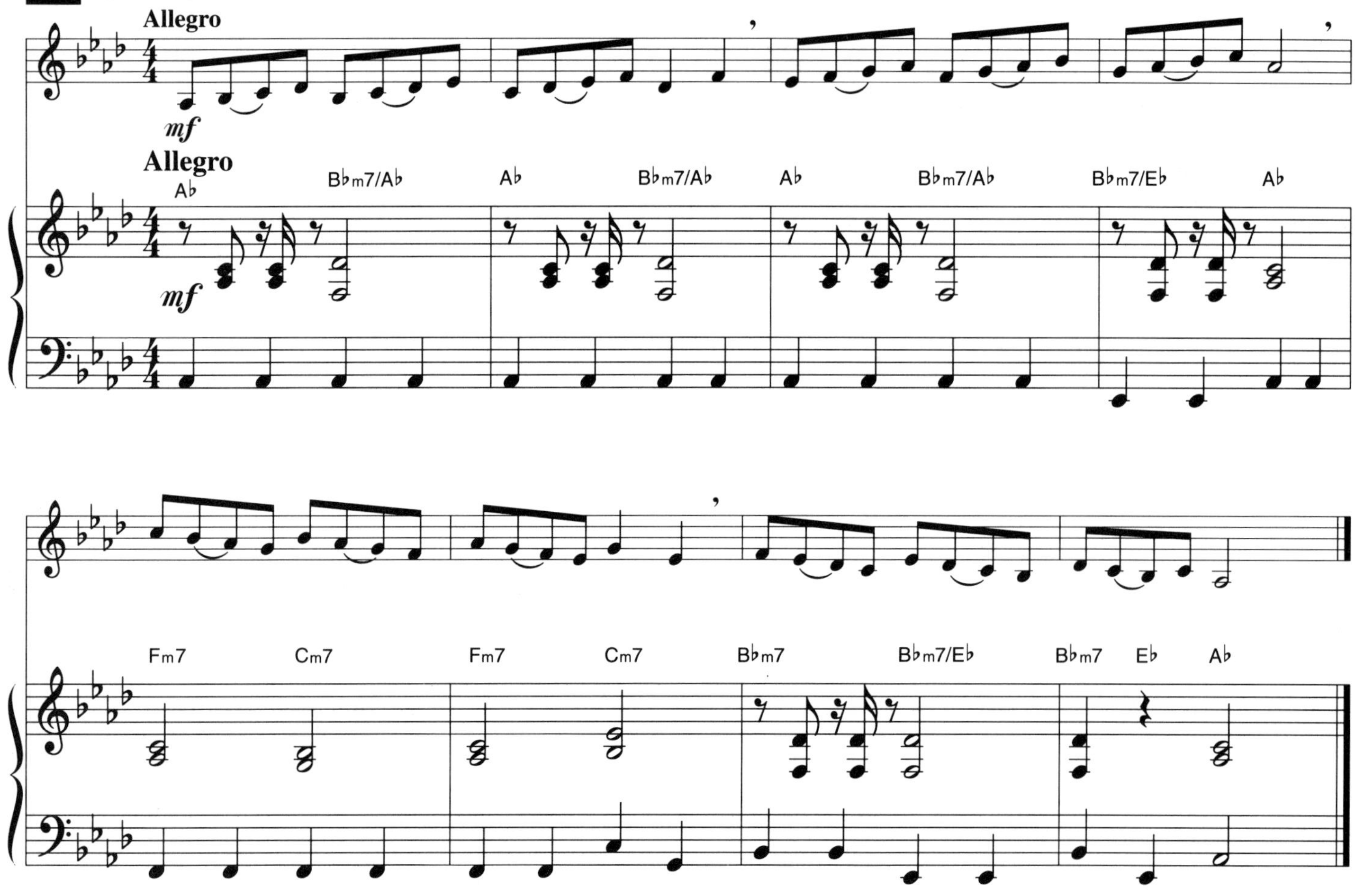

38 PARTNER SONGS - Duet

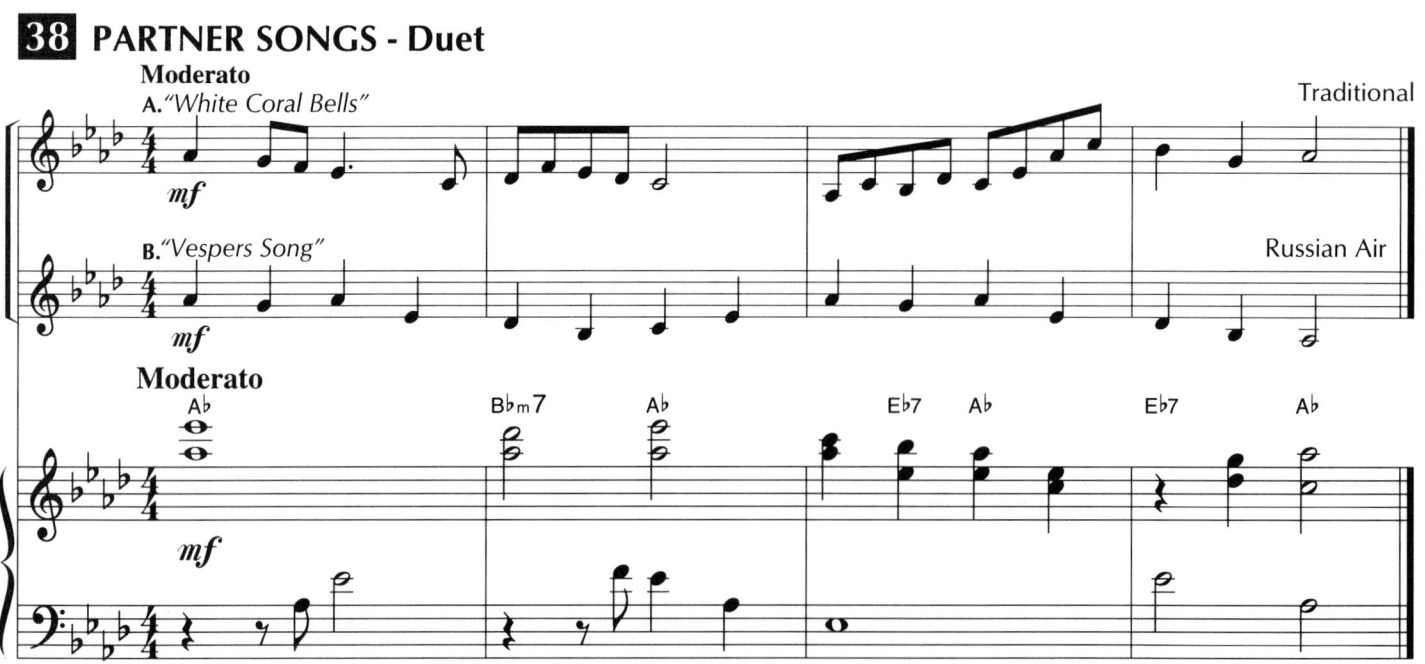

39 GO FOR EXCELLENCE!

Stephen Foster (1826 - 1864)

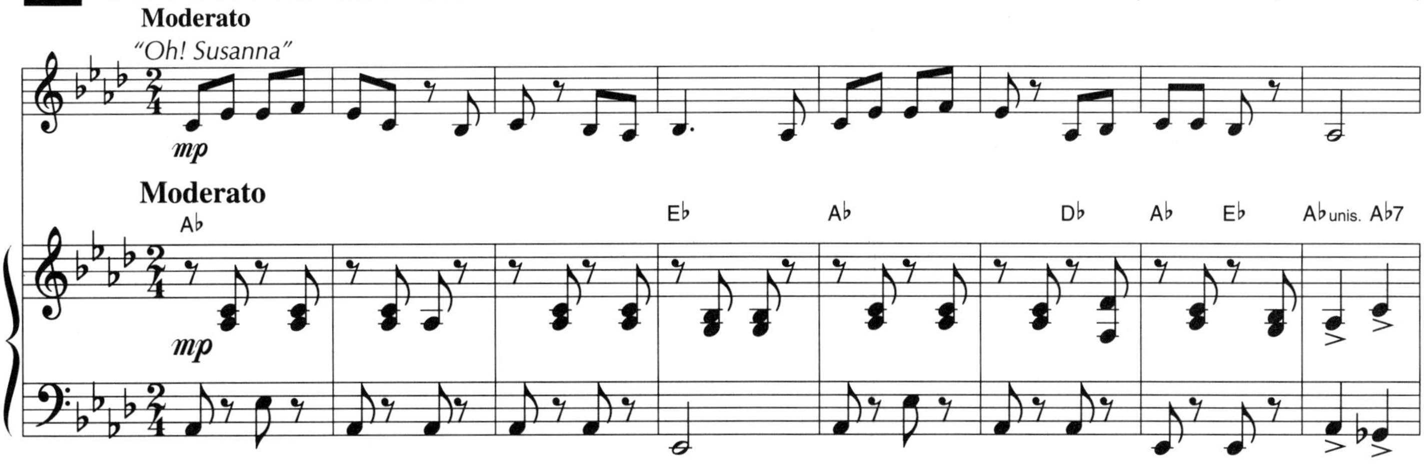

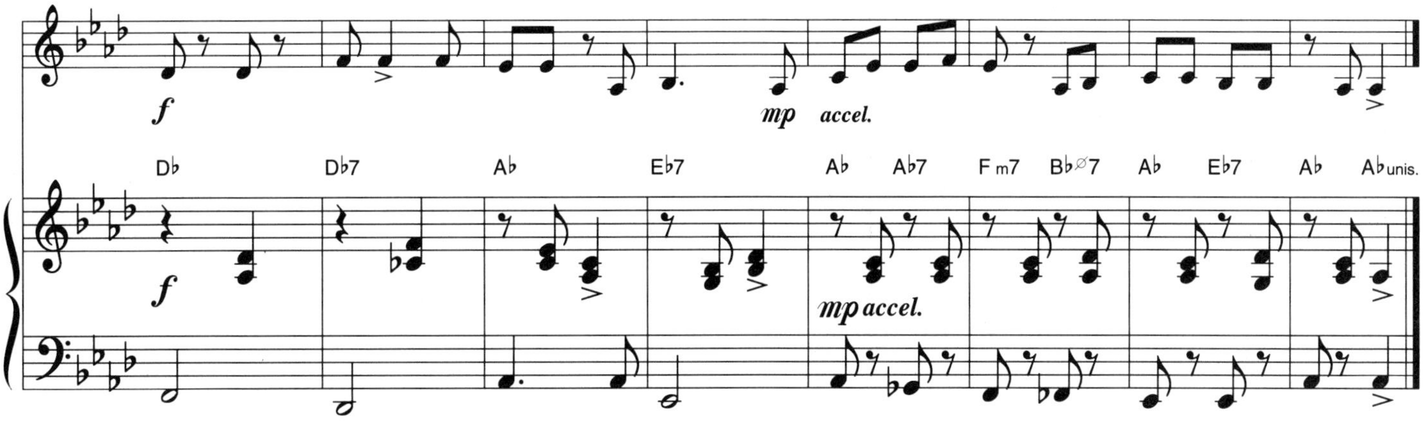

41 CHROMATIC CAPERS

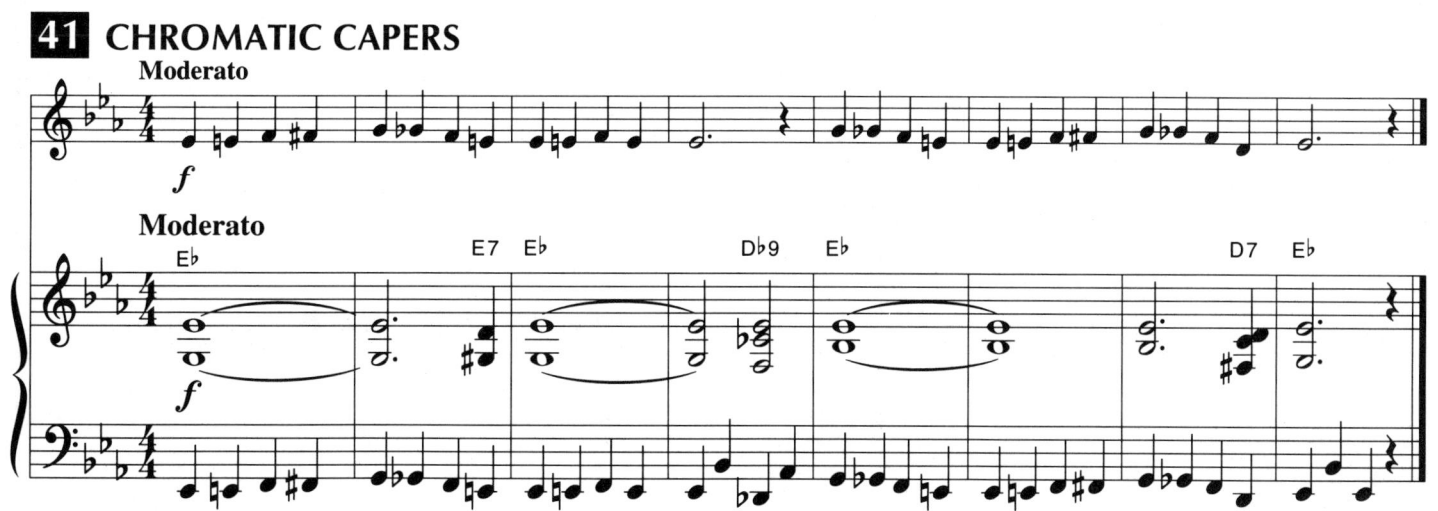

42 SHENANDOAH

American Folk Song

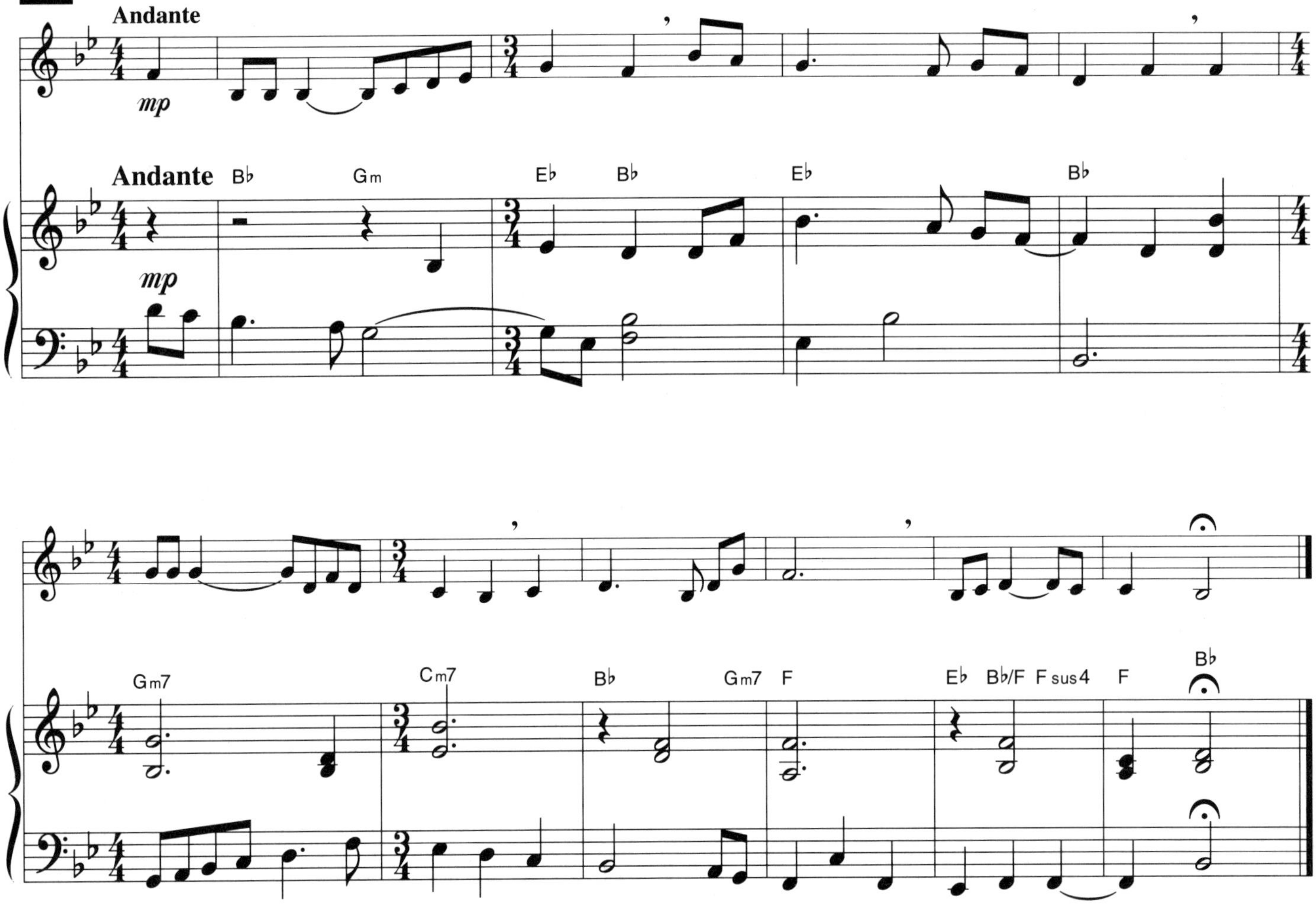

43 THEME FROM SYMPHONY NO. 94

Franz Joseph Haydn (1732 - 1809)

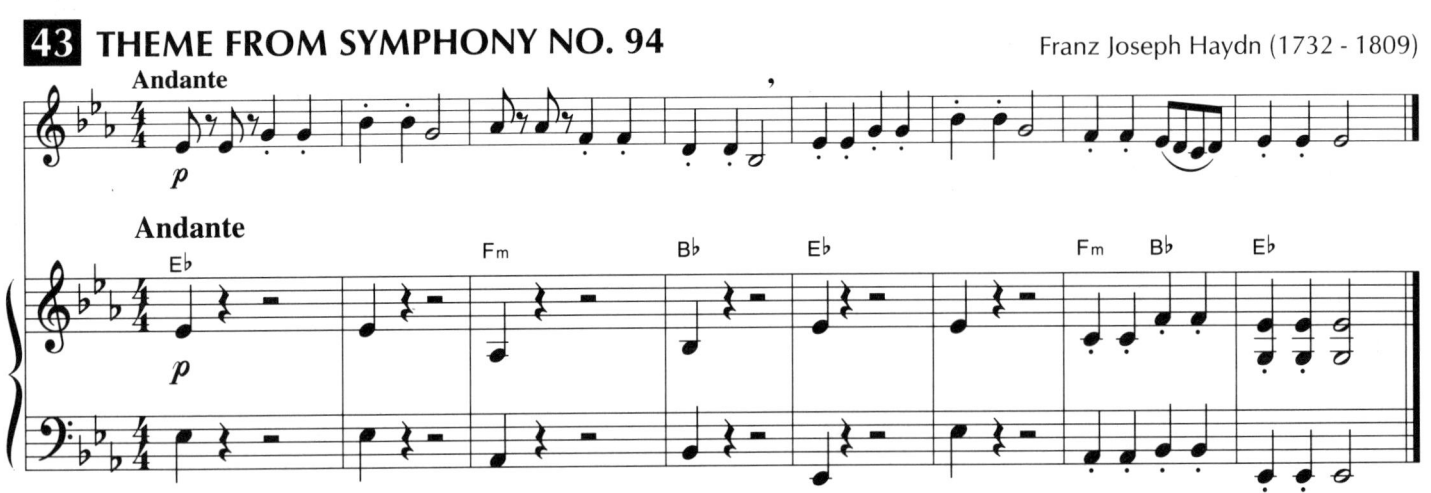

48 MARCHE SLAV

Peter Ilyich Tchaikovsky (1840 - 1893)

50 JUBILATE

Wolfgang Amadeus Mozart (1756 - 1791)

51 GO FOR EXCELLENCE!

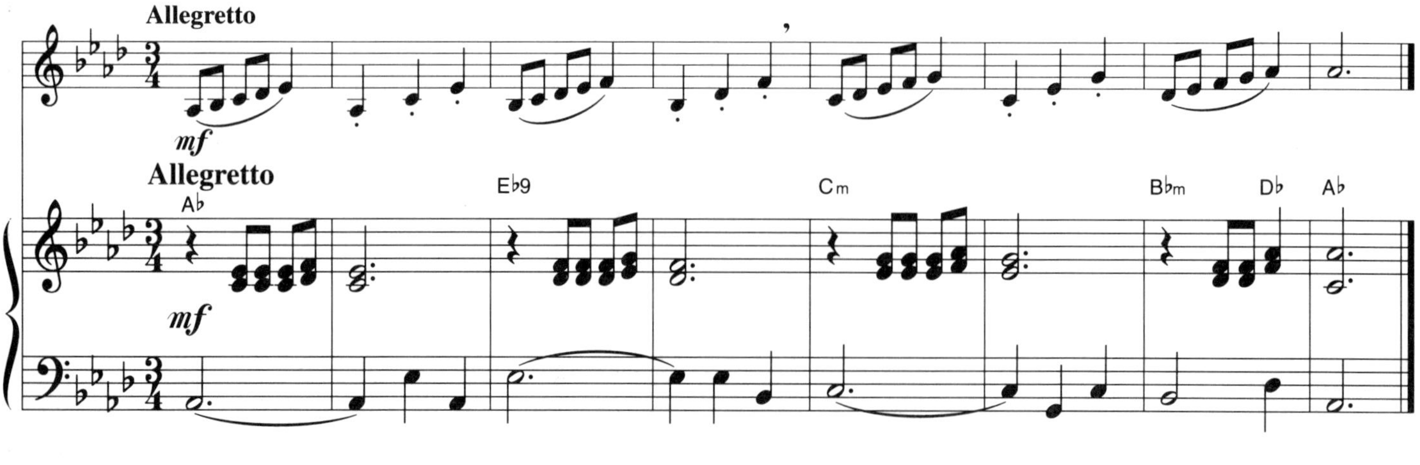

52 WARM-UP

53 HABAÑERA

Georges Bizet (1838 - 1875)

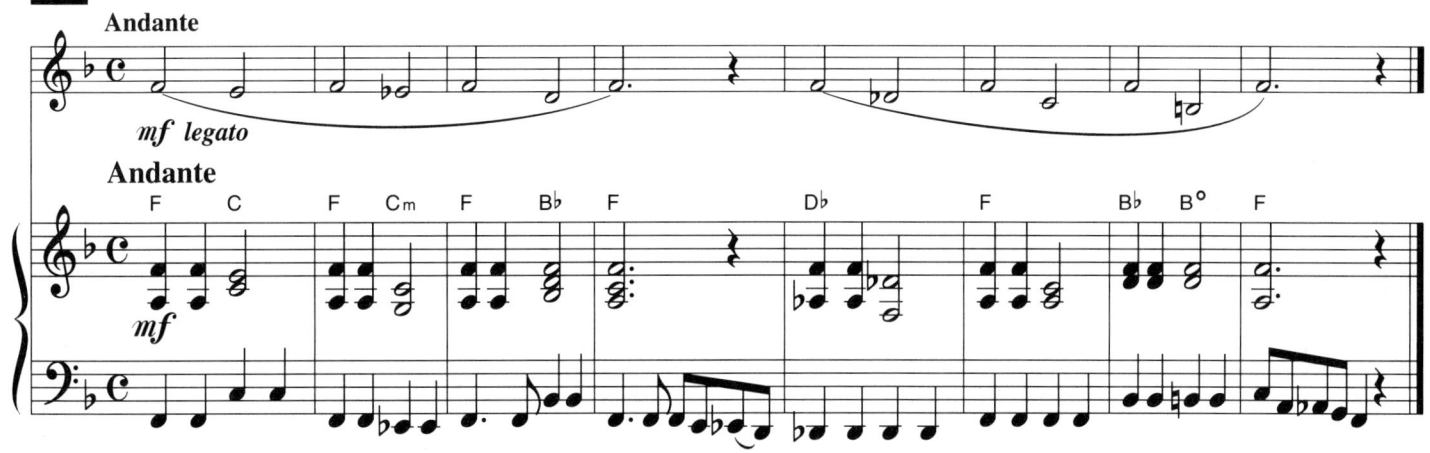

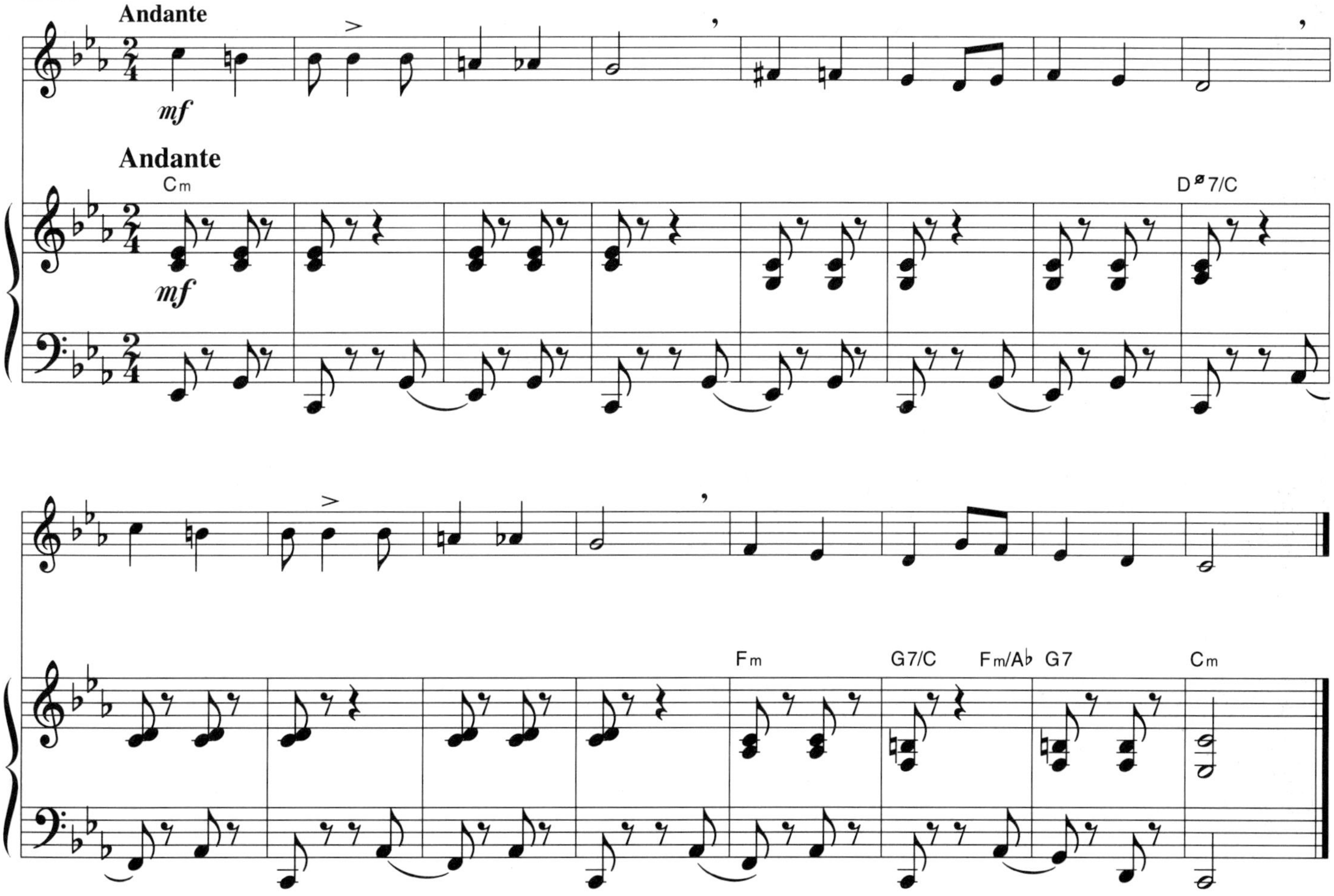

22

54 **SMOOTH AS SILK**

Allegretto

55 **HEY HO - Round (Canon)**

Medieval Song

Allegro

W22PG

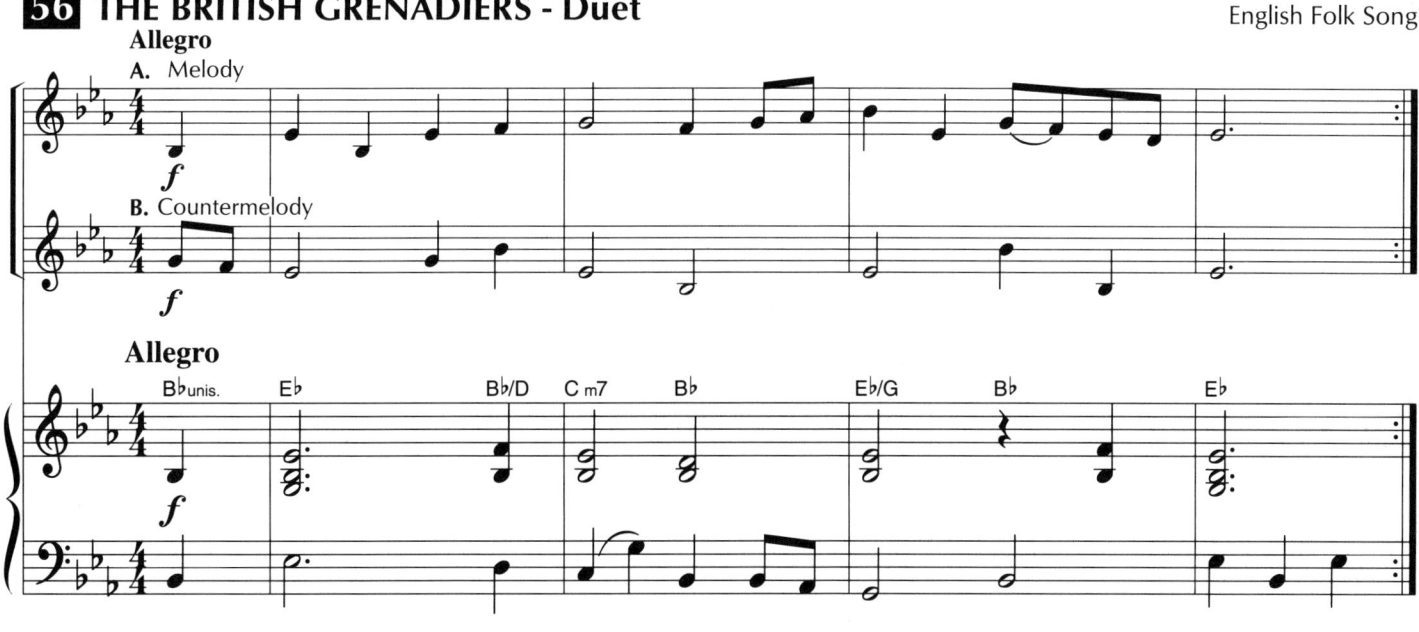
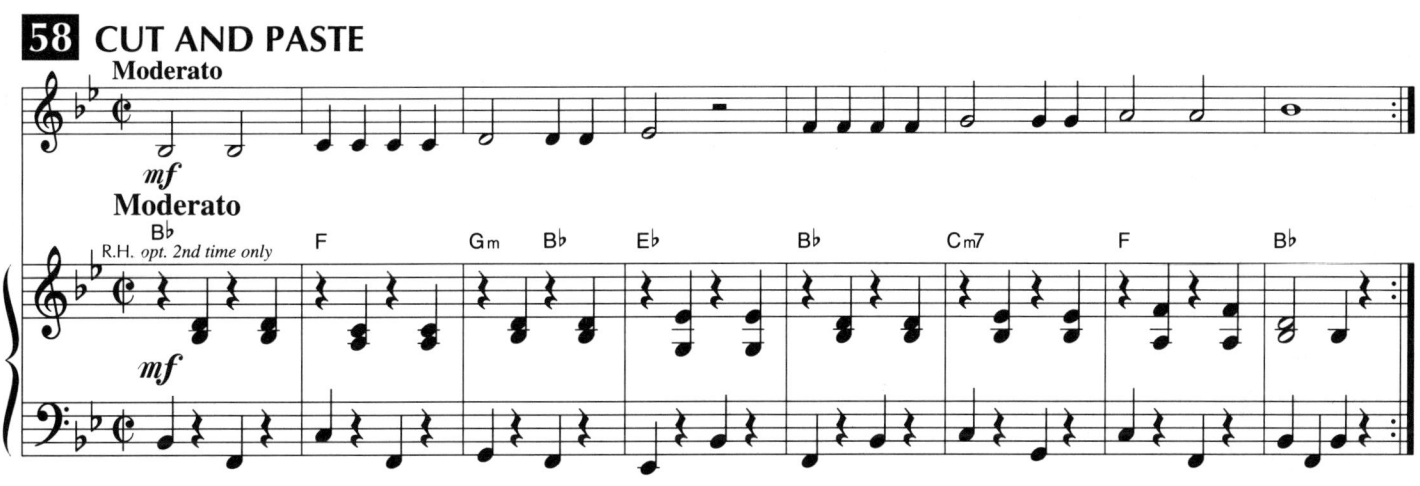

62. GO FOR EXCELLENCE!

John Philip Sousa (1854 - 1932)

Allegretto
"High School Cadets March"

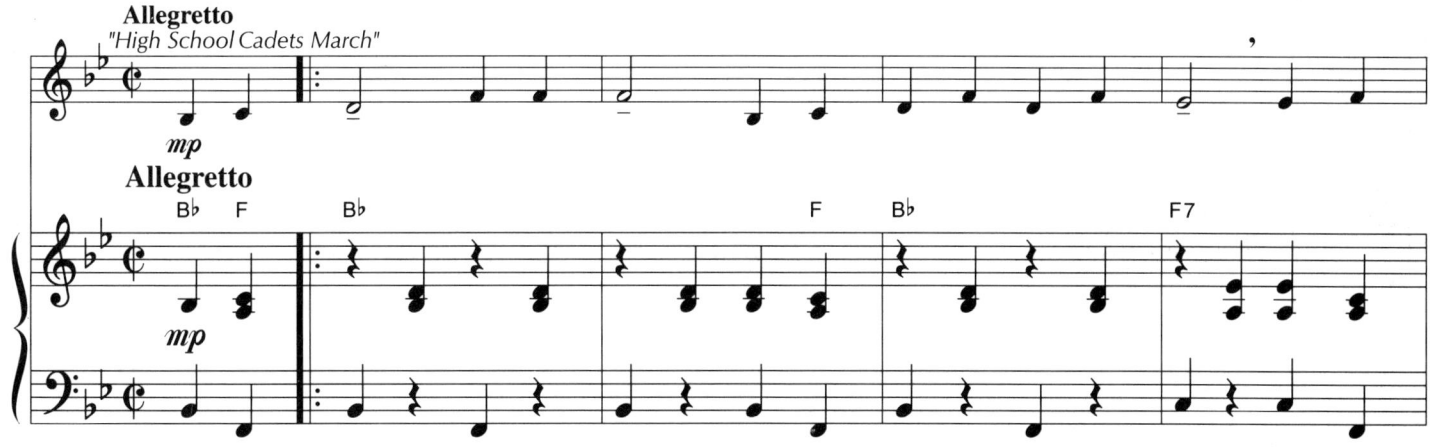
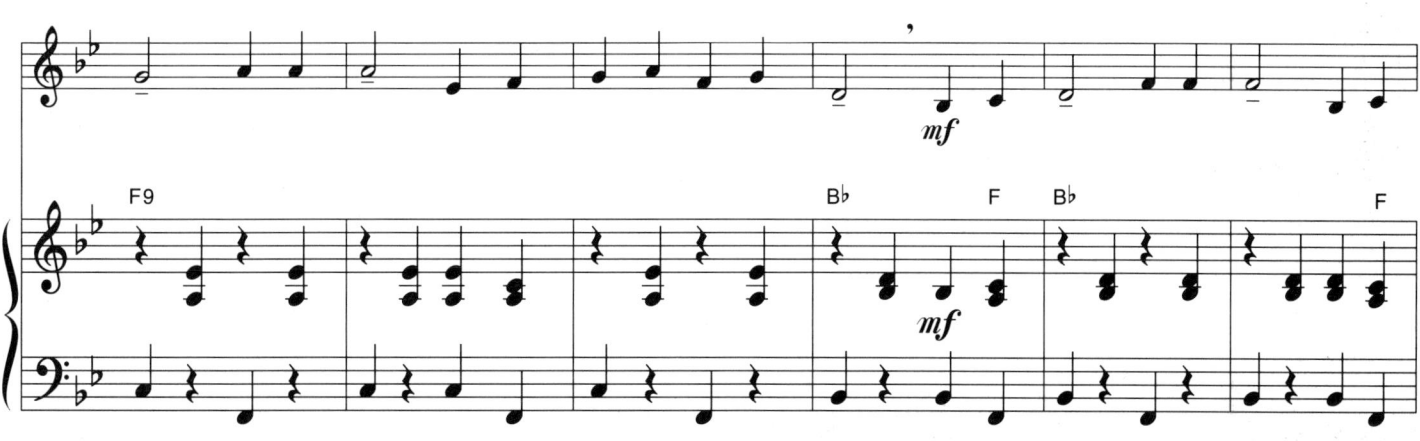

26

64 DANISH ROLL

Danish Folk Song

65 RUSSIAN SAILORS' DANCE

Reinhold Glière (1875 - 1956)

W22PG

68 CHROMATIC SCALE SKILL

69. SAILING THE HIGH SEAS

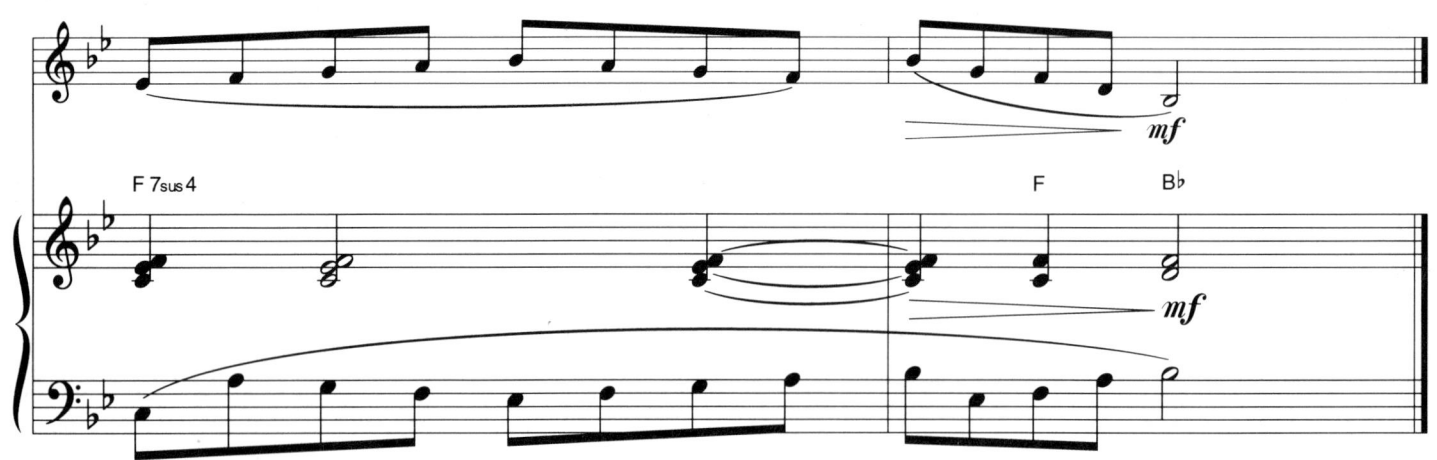

70 **CHROMATIC MARCH**

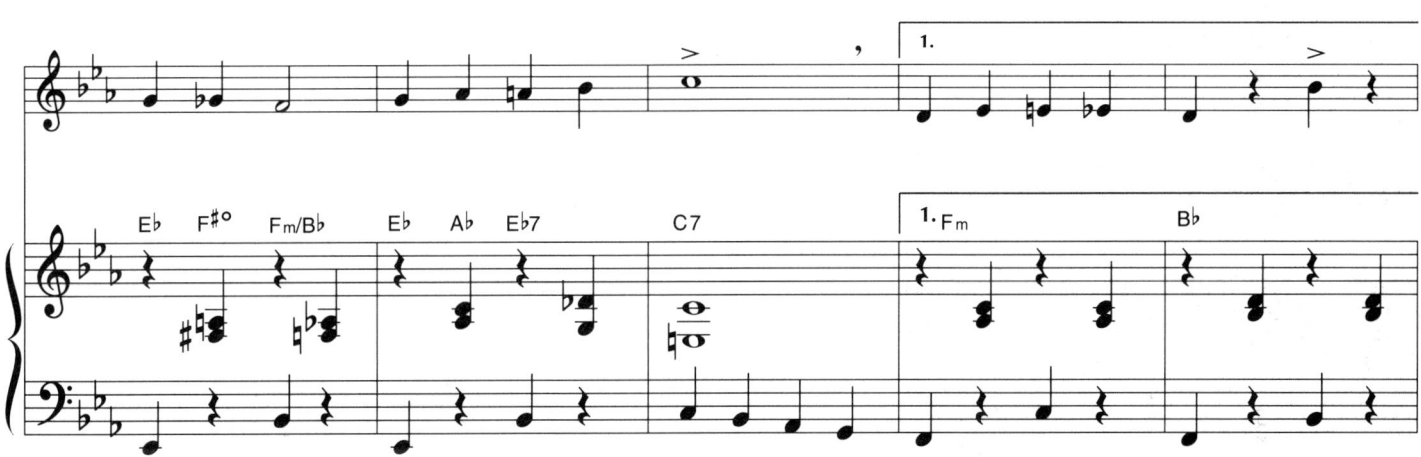

71. MANHATTAN BEACH MARCH

John Philip Sousa (1854 - 1932)

72 GO FOR EXCELLENCE!

74 TRIPLE PLAY

77 CONCERT C MAJOR SCALE SKILL

78 OVER THE RIVER
Traditional

87 GO FOR EXCELLENCE!

Patrick Gilmore (1829 - 1892)

"When Johnny Comes Marching Home"

88 LOOBY LOO

Anonymous

91 **GIVE MY REGARDS TO BROADWAY**

George M. Cohan (1878 - 1942)

94 **STEADY AS YOU GO - Duet**

95 **TIRRA LIRRA LOO**

Canadian Folk Song

96 **GO FOR EXCELLENCE!** American Folk Song

"Big Rock Candy Mountain"

TURKISH MARCH
from "The Ruins of Athens"

Solo with Piano Accompaniment

Ludwig van Beethoven (1770 - 1827)
arr. Bruce Pearson (b. 1942)

97 BLAZIN'

98 AMERICAN PATROL

Frank W. Meacham (1856 - 1909)

102 DOTS OF FUN

103 LITTLE BROWN JUG - Duet

Joseph Eastburn Winner (1837 - 1918)

108 MARCH MILITAIRE

Franz Schubert (1797 - 1828)

112 TRIPLE TREAT

113 STARS OF THE HEAVENS - Duet

Mexican Folk Song

114 LIGHT CAVALRY OVERTURE

Franz von Suppé (1819 - 1895)

115 GO FOR EXCELLENCE!

Charles Gounod (1818 - 1893)

"Soldiers' Chorus from Faust"

116 HERE WE COME A-WASSAILING

English Folk Song

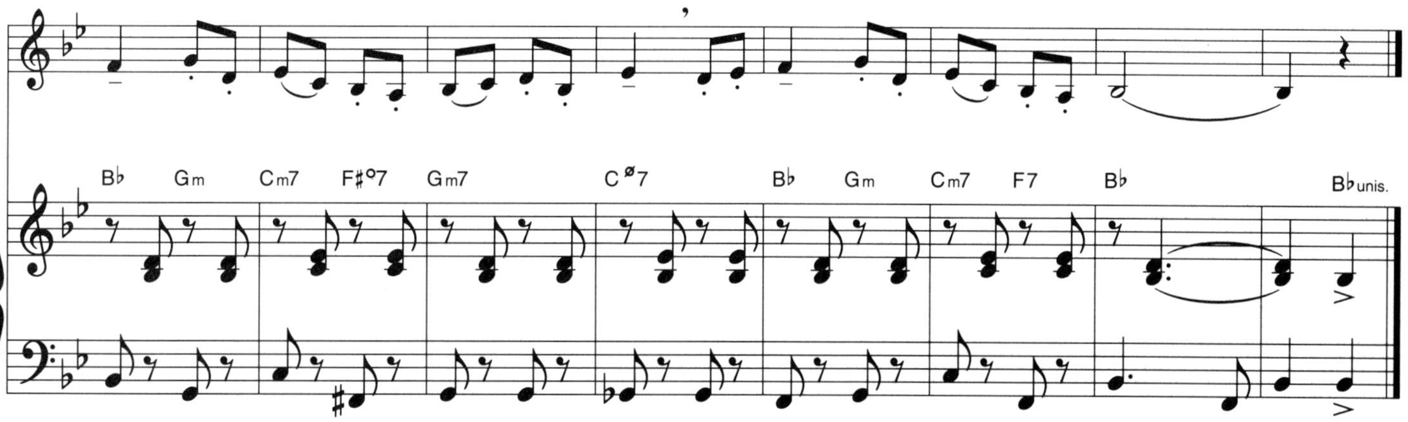

117 **THEME FROM "ZAMPA"**

Ferdinand Herold (1791 - 1833)

118 GO FOR EXCELLENCE!

Peter Ilyich Tchaikovsky (1840 - 1893)